SHOP CATS
OF
HONG KONG

Photographs by Marcel Heijnen
Haiku and cat stories by Ian Row

LABOUR, LUCK & LOVE

A glimpse into the curious world of
the city's coolest shop assistants

by Catharine Nicol

Fluffy or sleek, lithe or lazy, cats have kept us humans enraptured for centuries. Infamously aloof, fiercely independent and effortlessly enigmatic, they prowl, pounce and purr to their own tune.

Cats are the mysterious yin to dogs' gregarious yang, and we love them for it. The feline cold shoulder makes their sudden playful, affectionate and even clingy moments so much more delightful. You can never take a cat's behaviour for granted, and it is this unpredictability that keeps us in their mesmerizing power.

HISSTORY

It took many centuries to tame the cat, or perhaps to train the human to be a worthy owner. Earliest evidence suggests humans and cats cohabited as far back as 7500 BC. It is believed that the symbiotic relationship probably started around 10,000 years ago, when we humans first paused our nomadic hunting and gathering lifestyles. When we discovered agriculture, the storage of food and grain attracted rodents, initiating the start of the beautiful bond between farmer and feline.

Perhaps the ancient Egyptians were the most spellbound of all. During the 22nd Dynasty (c. 940 BC onwards), not only did they domesticate cats, they also elevated them to sacred status and worshipped them in the name of Bast or Bastet, defender of the Pharaoh and goddess of fertility. While cats protected food stores with their pest control skills, any human accused of killing one of these exalted animals faced the death penalty. And when the cats turned up their own furry paws, they were often mummified and buried alongside their owners, continuing the affectionate relationship into the afterlife.

Cats in Egypt became frequent sailors on ships cruising the Nile, and they didn't stop there. Ship's cats became popular around the world, preventing disease and damage to vessels and cargo by catching rodents. As a bonus, they served as company and entertainment for the crew. Legend has it that Christopher Columbus had cats aboard his ships, the *Niña*, the *Pinta* and the *Santa María*. It's easy to imagine explorers through the ages, mapping new-found lands with their moggies beside them – probably sitting on the parchment and smudging the ink, or tracking damp paw prints across it. In any case, it didn't take long before there were felines in every port, and cats started taking over the world.

Fast forward to the time when innovative inventions came to cement the symbiotic relationship between human and cat. As pets, cats were invited to share the luxury of living indoors, with humans altering their architecture to bring the outside in. As cats became permanent family members, catflaps and kitty litter (not to mention tinned cat food and neutering) became standard.

These days, the little hinged 'door-within-a-door' has been transformed into a high-tech chip-activated gadget. An entertaining legend claims the catflap was originally invented by none other than Sir Isaac Newton. The brilliant scientist allegedly didn't want to keep leaping up to open the door for Spithead, his indecisive four-footed friend, when he was in the middle of developing the laws of motion. Perhaps it was the closing of the catflap, rather than the falling of the apple, which provided the 'aha' moment that clarified his law of gravity.

FAMOUS CATS

Spithead is just one of many famous cats – or strictly speaking, cats with famous owners. Abraham Lincoln was the president who introduced the first cat into the White House, although it was the Clintons' cat Socks who earned the name 'First Cat of the United States' (although FCOTUS never caught on as a title).

A politicat across the water, Humphrey lived at 10 Downing Street between 1988 and 1997. Employed as the official Chief Mouser to the Cabinet Office, he outstayed Conservative Prime Ministers Margaret Thatcher and John Major, but retired under the Labour government of Tony Blair. The position of Chief Mouser is currently occupied by Larry, a former rescue cat who began his career under David Cameron in 2011 and has continued to serve under Theresa May and Boris Johnson.

We aren't all lucky enough to have homes with real cats, so fictional cats have long filled this feline-shaped hole. In the west, we love the Cheshire Cat from Lewis Carroll's *Alice in Wonderland* and many grew up with Dr Seuss's quirky *Cat in the Hat*. More recently, kids have followed the ups and downs of lasagne-loving Garfield, and who in today's world hasn't received some item festooned with a picture of the expressionless Hello Kitty?

Cats have created iconic moments on the silver screen, including the sweet cat named 'Cat' who starred alongside Audrey Hepburn in *Breakfast at Tiffany's*, the déjà-vu black cat from *The Matrix*, and angry Mrs Norris in the *Harry Potter* series. Villains seem drawn to cats, or do cats feel a wicked affiliation with villains? Don Vito Corleone showed his softer side by petting a tabby (actually a stray found on the Paramount lot) in *The Godfather*, while the white fluffy supervillain first seen with Blofeld in *From Russia with Love* was spoofed in *Austin Powers* by bald Mr Bigglesworth. Jonesey survived on board the Nostromo with Ellen Ripley in *Alien*, Goose in *Captain Marvel* turned out to have a startlingly scary side, while Puss in Boots in *Shrek 2* parodied the watery dance sequence from *Flashdance*.

Possibly the richest cat in the world was owned by the late Karl Lagerfeld. Choupette was a muse for the renowned designer, her elegance and attitude inspiring him daily. She accompanied him in ads and allegedly amassed a fortune of around €3 million.

MANEKI-NEKO, THE LUCKY CAT

Requiring neither a catflap nor kitty litter, Japan's ceramic *maneki-neko* or 'beckoning cat' is a firm fixture throughout south-east Asia. The earliest records mention these figurines as far back as the Edo Period (1603–1868). Often nicknamed the 'lucky cat', the *maneki-neko* usually wears a collar with a bell, has its left or right paw in the air, and holds a golden koban coin. Alternative adornments may include a drum, a fish, a fan, a gemstone or a money bag. These days, the *maneki-neko*'s one-pawed 'high five' often moves mechanically, endlessly swaying back and forth.

It is named the 'beckoning cat' because when the Japanese beckon, they do so with their arm held up and hand facing down, flapping their fingers. In the west, however, the most widespread beckoning gesture is arm down, hand facing up, so the cat is often said to be waving instead. Some think the gesture depicts a cat washing its face, which could mean either that a visitor is about arrive, or that's it's going to rain, both of which are believed to be lucky.

The meanings behind the gestures and colours are as contrary as the animal and depend upon where you are in the world. In general, however, it is believed a cat beckoning with its left paw brings new customers, making it ideal for a shop, while a cat beckoning with its right paw brings luck and wealth into the home. Occasionally you'll see both paws up, which means the cat is offering protection.

The original *maneki-neko* was white, symbolizing purity and good fortune, but more recently, Feng Shui-inspired colour variations have appeared. A black *maneki-neko* is said to banish evil spirits, a gold one attracts wealth, and red enhances relationships, while green is good for education and health, blue for wisdom, and pink for romance.

HONG KONG'S SHOP CATS

The real cats in this book are certainly believed by their owners to be lucky. In some city neighbourhoods like Sheung Wan and Sai Ying Pun, where businesses date back generations, you'll find almost every local dried goods shop has a cat. Owners believe the mere smell of a cat heralds danger to mice, so even if the – ahem – less young and fit among them have retired from hunting, simply being in residence can be enough.

While some were deliberately acquired by the shop owners for their mousing skills, other shops were adopted by the cats, who just turned up one day and made themselves at home.

However they arrived, each quickly became an essential part of the life, the business and the family in the shops where they live and hunt. The shop owners, without exception, have grown to love their feline friends, not only for the company they offer day in, day out, but also for their business skills.

Shop life may look somewhat laid back in these pages, but rest assured, business is always taken seriously in Hong Kong. The cats, especially the playful ones, bring customers into the shop by enlivening the atmosphere and providing a friendly welcome. They create an extra bond with the public and may even exert some of their mysterious influence in boosting sales. It seems the cats' lucky reputation is more than just a legend.

CATS WILL BE CATS

Wherever you are in the world, cats do what cats do. They live their lives on their own terms, even in the semi-formal public space that is a shop.

In Marcel's photographs, you'll see them grooming themselves any time, anywhere – on the counter, one leg akimbo, without a care in the world. They monopolize the scales used for weighing ingredients and sprawl on the till, making it hard to add up bills. They stare unblinkingly at their human's lunch, waiting for a treat, or they retreat, peering out from piles of dried fish, or catnapping on top of rice sacks. And of course they frequently ignore everything and everyone, self-sufficient in their own little world.

The relationship between owner and cat is a highlight within these images. Waves of telepathic communication emanate from the page, whether scathing criticisms and cheeky remarks or mutual appreciation and true love.

Ian Row's astute haiku brilliantly put words to the cats' innermost thoughts. The feline insights into their owners and shop life are delivered in a suitably deadpan style. Nonchalance meets humour, but always with a whisker of affection. Even where owner and cat are looking in different directions, their expressions suggest they might thinking the same thing. Are they really in synch, laughing at the folly of life, or engaging in a passive-aggressive sulk over office politics?

CATS & CULTURE

Marcel's captivating images also give us fascinating glimpses of the Chinese territory of Hong Kong. Beautifully framed, the layers of detail are sometimes anchored by the shop owner or the cat, and sometimes by the minutiae of the shop itself.

Culture and commerce come together in these colourful and often chaotic interiors, stacked with products. They tell the story of customs that go back centuries, ranging from traditional Chinese medicine stores and shops selling paper offerings for the dead to those stacked with mysterious towers of boxes.

Some cats and their owners or shops seem almost to look like one another. Did they grow to resemble each other in attitude, colouring and facial expression after so many years of co-habitation?

Sometimes you can't help but wonder how Marcel even spotted the cats that blend in with all the clutter in the background. Is it a coincidence that a tortoiseshell cat lives in a shop filled with mottled old boxes, a ginger cat sits in front of red offerings, or a grey cat almost disappears into the dust?

Whether it takes you a while to spot the shop cats within these pages, or whether they are staring straight at you, one thing is clear; there are no rats here.

If you ever visit Hong Kong, make sure to wander the streets of Sheung Wan and Sai Ying Pun and when you see a cat sitting sentry in a shop, stop to say hello – it just might be one of the famous felines featured in this book.

A NOTE ON THE HAIKU

The traditional (Japanese) haiku is made up of 3 lines and 17 *sounds*. Sounds in the Japanese language are not equivalent to syllables in English. For example, the word 'haiku' is two syllables in English (*hi-ku*), but three *sounds* in Japanese (*ha-i-ku*). So the 5-7-5 syllable rule is effectively a Western imposition and places excessive emphasis on form. What's essential in writing haiku is the development – some would say the 'unfolding' – of a story. The haiku in this book therefore pay homage to the traditional short–long–short format, as opposed to following a strict 5-7-5 structure, while staying true to the spirit of the poetic form.

RE:TAIL THERAPY

by Marcel Heijnen

In late 2015 I found myself based in Hong Kong again after an 18-year hiatus, and living without a cat for the first time in about 40 years.

Luckily, the Sai Ying Pun area that I moved to had plenty of feline distractions and soon I was on first-name basis with a number of them. Dau Ding was the first one I spotted during a morning walk. I paused for a while, snapped a quick photo, and moved on... only to find yet another kitty a few shops down the road. And then another one. It took only a few more of these encounters for me to realize there was a potential series there. So here it is.

Yes, it's about the cats – but it's just as much about the context: these chaotic yet organically organized shops are beautiful photogenic subjects in their own right. These are places where time seems to stand still, devoid of all the branding and modern-day retail trickery to which we've grown accustomed.

The cats are essential to the photo series, but sometimes a feline just becomes an excuse to shoot a particular shop – an ice-breaker that gives me a reason to smile at the shop owner and have a little chat before I press the shutter.

In most modern cities there will be all kinds of rules and regulations against cats in shops. Not in Hong Kong, and I'm grateful for that. Here we can still witness this wonderful symbiotic relationship between human and feline. The reasons for it hark back to why we first domesticated cats centuries ago: mouse-catching and companionship.

I hope you'll enjoy looking at these photographs as much as I enjoyed taking them. Some of the subjects have names, including Fei Zai, Siu Faa and Ah Tai, while others might as well be called Wally. You'll see why – go and find them!

PS: No animals were harmed during the making of this book.

I am sooo hungry

Leave some for me, greedy

You can afford to

Too hot, too humid

Too hard to do anything

Too lazy to lunch

Give him a moment
I'd help out, but I don't have
opposable thumbs

Excuse me, I'm working

Very important job

Quality control

Dinner time, he says

I'll have noodles, says the cat

Handmade and homemade

Humans need softness

Natural or synthetic

Cat sleeps standing up

Sleeves rolled, legs stretched
Open for business
Can I help you?

Suffice it to say
she does her best work from
inside the box

I'm not just his cat
I'm his wife, I chose to return
to watch over him

A man and his cat
in sympathy, yet minding
their own business

An easy silence

Years of practice and knowing

I know him by heart

The humans focus
on suits and pairs; a cat reflects
on bigger things

One day, he will fall

Use a ladder, I say, but

they never listen

DAU DING
(LITTLE BEAN)

The Gracious Host

I was a rough and tumble alley cat when my owners found me. I had heard about 'the good life', where you didn't have to worry about where your next meal was coming from and where you were sleeping that night, so I didn't resist when they 'rescued' me, brought me home and quickly put me to work as 'security cat' at their shop.

Life on the streets was tough but this new job is hard work. So many mice, so little time! But I was committed. Day in and day out, I did my duty – keeping the shop free of mice. And I'm proud to say, I managed it without killing a single mouse. See, when you come from the streets, you realize everyone is just trying to survive, even the mice. People say mice are pests but some of my best friends are mice. And you don't eat your friends! So to keep my owners happy, I pretend to chase the mice away. But I let them stay because even mice need a place to belong. And I even share my rice and bonito flakes – my favourite meal – with them.

So while my owners refer to me as their furry little security guard, my little friends call me the Gracious Host.

DAU DING

DAU DING

Presiding over your
weaknesses, your secrets
Business of healing

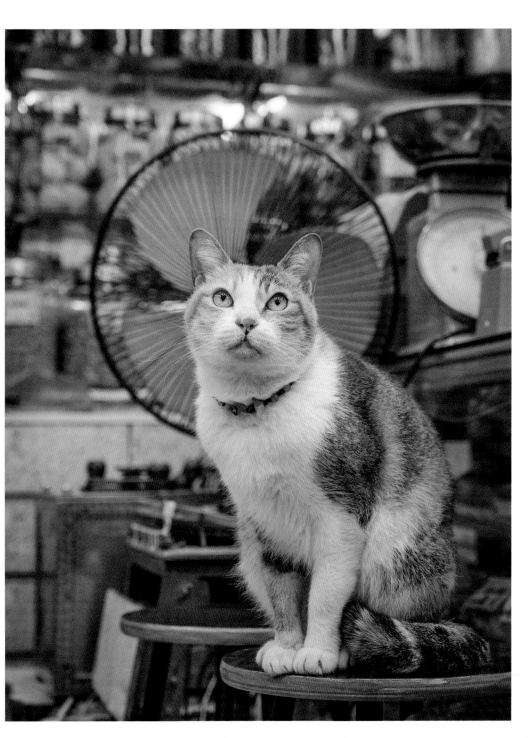

Heard the one about

the cat that got stuck in the plastic tub?

It didn't end well

Her royal highness

A walk to meet her people

Every now and zen

I'll have some ribs

Shoulder, cheeks and belly, please

Thanks, Uncle Porky

Hey, stop that racket!

Can't you see I'm sleeping here?

Leave my lunch and go

That was yummy

I'd do it all over again

but I'm so little

The weight of the world
and today's headlines drive her
to the brink of nap

She's crazy

Not just today but ALL THE TIME

Help me

This is the last straw
Next time you're late and don't call
you're grounded – for life!

And for my next trick:

My head – on the chopping block!

Move me closer

People think it's him
who brings in the business, but
I do all the work

Two eyes good, four eyes
better: that's the golden rule
Cover all bases

潔淨進行中

CLEANING
PROGRESS

'Cleaning in progress'
Cat will resume transmission
in due course

I don't mind lizards
Closer to birds than you think
I don't mind birds

I'll make you a deal
Buy one and I'll throw in a
small one for your cat

Into her ear

he whispers sweet nothings

Marry me

Suspended in air
Mind over matter or a
matter of balance?

Some animals, more

likely to be ornamental

The luck of the draw

AH DAI
(NUMBER ONE)

The Retired Mouser

When I took up residence at the rice shop eight years ago, the agreement I had with the owner was simple – I would apprehend all the cheeky mice and stop them from stealing from the stock and in return, I would get a room and meals. I thought it was a good deal.

The first few years went by without any hitches or complaints. Then one day, *out of the blue,* I stopped. Just like that. Enough! I simply thought 'why am I working so hard?' There's more to life than being caught up in the rat race. What I did enjoy was the charming neighbourhood, the regular meals from the owner – plus the secret snacks from the next-door neighbours – and my comfy 'gunny sack in a cardboard box' bed, of course. Around the same time, my owner took ill and started to require more attention. You know how needy humans can get. But I felt sorry for him and besides, I wasn't doing anything else. So I upped the frequency of my visits, and increased the amount of snuggles, cuddles and kisses. It's the least I can do.

AH DAI

AH DAI

Half you see me
half you don't; I'm invisible
if I just stay still

Let's try something new:
how to think outside the box
without stepping out

〈Y.C〉余昌中西藥行
品名 花旗參
每両 90, 元

〈Y.C〉余昌中西藥行
品名 靚石斛

中西藥行

香港名牌
HONG KONG TOP BRAND

10,000 years

Generations later

One in a million

Where did my youth go?
I once had style, grace and form
Now I've just got form

I've thought about it

You know... about leaving this place

But where will I go?

Shop for rent

Rates included/long term lease

No dogs permitted

Closed on Sunday
I'm still not used to
being left behind

I think I like you
I know we've only just met
Take my hand

You don't know me
But do you need to know me
to love me?

Goodbye, pawn shop

You're not my 'forever home'

Time to move on

This looks familiar

Years may pass, you don't forget

Looking for mother

Up above, she waits

Down below, we try to guess

Where she's going next

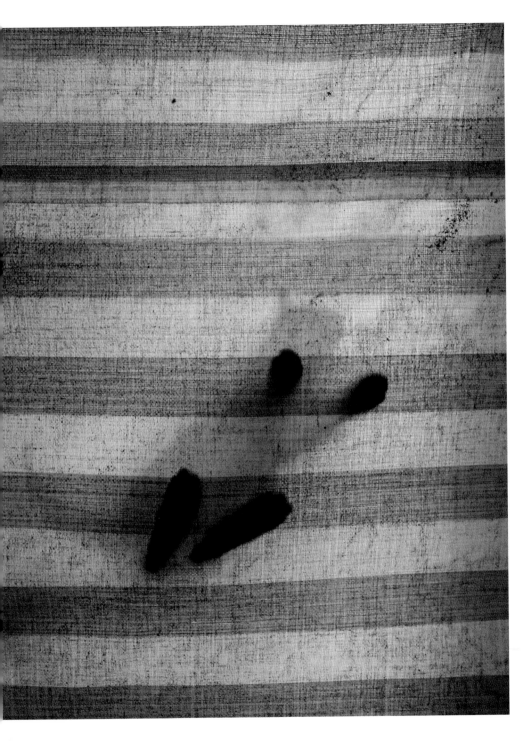

Your superstitions

It's not easy being black

Water runs deep

FEI ZAI
(FAT BOY)

The Godfather

According to my owner, I was a little kitten when he found me in a small park. No one would have imagined that I would be destined for greatness. Apparently I was a mischievous little kitty and I would often get in trouble for stealing dried oysters, scallops and abalone from him. Who would have thought, ten years later I'd be a shrewd and successful businesscat, running a major business operation. You see, along the way, I discovered that I had a knack for buying and selling and I could smell an opportunity from miles away. There was excess stock and I knew the wealthy socialite cats – you know the types – who would pay good money for a superior product. So I recruited a few agents to help me grow this side of the business and I now preside over the largest black market trade in dried seafood south of the river. We sell off all our produce, don't pay as much tax – owner is happy. I get my 10% – I'm happy. I'm a genius! I may also have said too much. As a matter of fact, if I were you, I wouldn't repeat what I just told you to anyone or there could be... repercussions, if you know what I mean?

FEI ZAI

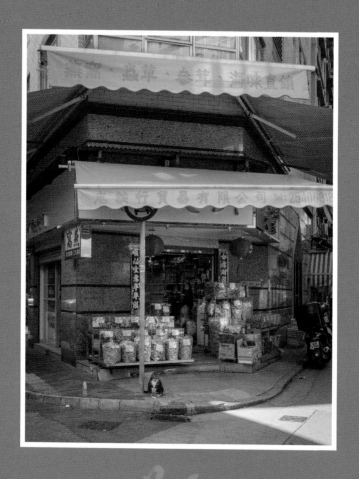

FEI ZAI

Cat 101
It's a mistake to assume
or ascribe meaning

They hear everything
even when they're asleep
Never trust the tail

Psst. Over here.

Help, I'm in the bottle!

Oh no. Can't. Breathe.

I print, he faxes
This office won't run itself
without clear guidelines

Twin brothers

Double, double toil and trouble

Plotting mischief

Those slippers aren't mine

And if they were, I wouldn't

leave them on the eggs

Watch the world go by
Waiting for something or nothing
Anything will do

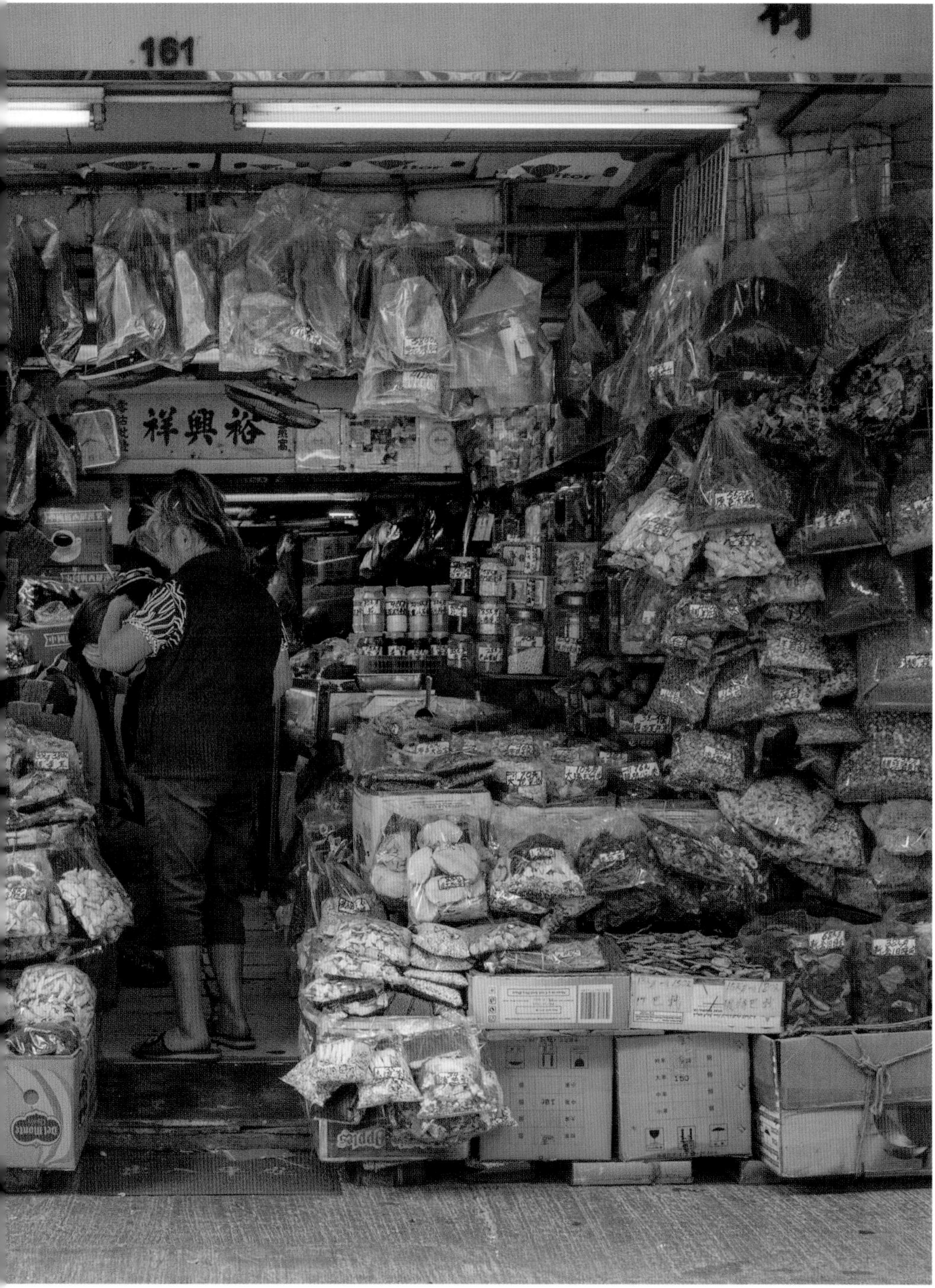
161
裕興祥

A cat's worst nightmare
Just too many choices in
hard-to-reach places

Seven samurai
Housebound but house-trained
Ready for battle

One thing I do know
Without cooking oil, 'fried stuff'
is just 'stuff'

This is my last round

Nothing will bring me back, not

even a paper doll

Ian Row was born and raised in Singapore and now lives in Melbourne, Australia. Ian has written haiku since 2006, when he realised how useful the form was in helping him exist in the present moment. He writes for Hot Cross Haiku.

First published in Hong Kong in 2016 under the title
Hong Kong Shop Cats by Asia One, Hong Kong

First published in the United Kingdom in 2021 by
Thames & Hudson Ltd, 181A High Holborn, London, WC1V 7QX

Reprinted 2024

Photography and design by Marcel Heijnen
www.chinesewhiskers.com, Instagram: @chinesewhiskers
Haiku and cat stories by Ian Row
Twitter: @ hotcrosshaiku, Instagram: @ianrow_hotcrosshaiku
Foreword by Catharine Nicol
Calligraphy by Mark Chan 墨山, www.markchan.com
Author photograph by Aleksander Solum

British Library Cataloguing-in-Publication Data
A catalogue record for this book is available from the British Library

ISBN   978-0-500-29623-3

Printed and bound in China by 1010 Printing International Ltd

Be the first to know about our new releases,
exclusive content and author events by visiting
thamesandhudson.com
thamesandhudsonusa.com
thamesandhudson.com.au